A SOMEWHAT OPTIMISTIC BOOK OF SPELLS FOR EMERGENCY USE WHEN ALL CONVENTIONAL METHODS OF CRISIS RESOLUTION HAVE FAILED

Author: Claire Taylor
Managing Editor: Simon Melhuish
Series Editor: Lee Linford
Design: Alan Shiner
Illustrations: Gary Sherwood
Additional contributor: Christine Pountney

Designed and compiled by
Mad Moose Press
for
Lagoon Books
PO Box 311, KT2 5QW, UK
PO Box 990676, Boston, MA 02199, USA

ISBN: 1-904139-28-0

www.madmoosepress.com
www.lagoongames.com

Printed in Hong Kong

A SOMEWHAT OPTIMISTIC BOOK OF SPELLS FOR EMERGENCY USE WHEN ALL CONVENTIONAL METHODS OF CRISIS RESOLUTION HAVE FAILED

Your partner just ran off with your best friend's mother shortly after breakfast, leaving you with her dreaded poodle. The office photocopier has been possessed by demonic administration gremlins and your boss has just canceled all vacations.

What's more, you're having a really bad hair day and the gargantuan, throbbing pustule at the end of your nose appears to be swelling by the hour, explosion imminent around the time that you bump into the cute, single, straight guy from the purchasing department.

All sounding a little too familiar? Then this book was written for you. Yes YOU! It comes packed with ingenious solutions to many of life's little problems and some of the bigger ones too.

Although the spells are virtually guaranteed to prove ineffectual, they should at least give you a good giggle. If not, you're probably suffering from a sense of humour deficiency. (This is not our fault and unfortunately there is no magical fix for such a severe condition.)

MAGIC TO USE...

To end a bad relationship 6
After an office party 8
On your driving examiner 10
In a nightclub 12
On a messy room 14
On the in-laws 16
To win on a slot machine 18
Whilst photocopying 20
On a beach holiday 22
In the kitchen 24
To get a pay rise 26
When waiting for a bus 28
On your waistline 30
In a two-fingered typing situation 32
When you're feeling down 34
Whilst doing the laundry 36
On the apple of your eye 38
To cover your tracks 40
In the bathroom 42
On unruly underwear 44
On a competition entry 46
Against a love rival 48
To deter unwanted e-mail 50
When laughter is required 52
On a bad complexion 54
On a suspect partner 56
At Christmas 58
To avenge the hairdresser 60
In a supermarket line-up 62
During an exam 64
For winning lottery numbers 66
During an argument 68
On thinning hair 70
On a run in your tights 72
To find lost things 74
On a snoring partner 76
On withering plants 78
To find a parking space 80
When you're feeling ill 82
If you're late 84
If you're weak-willed 86
When your shoes stink 88
On noisy people 90
On stressed people 92
To rekindle an old flame 94

SPELL

to end a relationship

To cut all ties
And make it quick,
Rub elbow thrice,
Give hair a flick,

Raise your foot
And point your toe,
Declaim aloud
Heave-ho, heave-ho!

Free me from
This pain and strife!
Make him vanish
From my life!

SPELL-CASTING TIP:

Perform this ritual whilst wearing suitably sturdy boots and standing on a photograph of the man in question.

Good men can be hard to find.
Perhaps it's time to join Mad Moose Speed Dating™

SPELL

to erase a colleague's memory of the office party

Spirit of Lager, Spirit of Gin,
Double-faced Spirits of pleasure and sin,

Spirits that with my restraint have toyed,
Drown any memories into the void.

Come, Spirits, and let vision be masked,
Blushes be spared, embarrassment finish.

Cloud, fog and haze all that has passed
Dim, Dimin, Dimini, Diminish!

SHOULD THE MAGIC FAIL:

Start checking the jobs section of your local newspaper.

Morning after essentials for any embarrassing office party.

CHARM
to pass your driving test

Examiner, Examiner,

Be filled with stamina

For during this next testing hour

You will remain under my power.

You will not see the ten-point turn,

You will not hear the gearbox burn,

You will not see me scrape a wall,

You will not hear my engine stall.

My smart manoeuvres will impel

You to free me from this dreaded 'L'.

SHOULD THE MAGIC FAIL:

Take the bus.

Iguanas: bad drivers, harsh examiners.

SPELL

to outshine a stunning friend in a nightclub

Mirror, Mirror, on the wall,

Who shows two friendly faces fair,

I command you in my thrall,

To make the fairest, her fairness share.

Mirror, Mirror, on the wall,

When we gyrate for all to see

Beneath the mirrored glitter ball,

Reflect her glory onto me.

SPELL-CASTING TIP:

Casually whisper this spell whilst re-applying make-up in the ladies' washroom, in the presence of the gorgeous one.

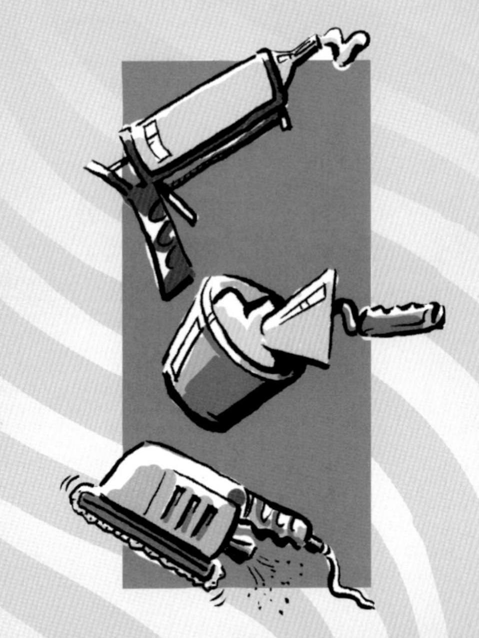

Don't waste time on this spell if your beauty regime involves using any or all of the above.

SPELL

for instant tidiness

Pandora, gaze upon this chaos
And pity us within.

Pandora, make this muddled bedlam
As neat as a shiny new pin.

Duster, polish, brush and broom,
Pigsty transmute into a room!

Papers, toys and dirty socks,
Pandora! Shut them in your box!

SHOULD THE MAGIC FAIL:

Shovel everything under the bed.

In extreme situations, move house.

Always check your vacuum cleaner for small children, pets and door-to-door salesmen.

CHARM

to charm the in-laws

Mother and father of the law,

This cup of tea which I now pour,

Shall soothe and calm all waters troubled,

And bring us all blessings doubled.

See my talents, not my flaws,

And in return, I won't see yours.

I am to you another child,

I shall forget the fact you drive me wild.

And when we all have drained our cups

We will behave like good grown-ups.

SHOULD THE MAGIC FAIL:

Offer to make another pot of tea - time spent in the kitchen is time spent avoiding arguments.

The In-law Endurance Kit™.

INCANTATION

to hit the jackpot on a slot machine

Nudge, nudge, wink, wink,
Wheels within wheels turn.

Clink, clink, chink, chink,
The time is nigh for me to earn.

Align thyselves with no tilting,
Fruit stand proud with no wilting,

Clink, clink, chink, chink,
My last dime I'm about to see,

Nudge, nudge, wink, wink
Give forth bountifully!

SHOULD THE MAGIC FAIL:

Quit before you need to remortgage the house and sell your partner's belongings.

Spare cash from gambling windfalls may be sent to the editor's retirement fund. All donations gratefully received.

MANTRA

to tame the photocopier

Gremlins, that in this copier dwell,
Thou shalt now fall aslumber.
Thou shalt let this machine work well
And copy precisely the right number.

Thy eyes shall close tight and fast,
No longer shalt thou caper.
The toner cartridge now will last,
Be gone the jams of paper.

All copies to be of intended size.
Gremlins, gremlins, I hypnotize!

SHOULD THE MAGIC FAIL:

Delegate the copying to the office junior. If you are the office junior, give the copier a good thump and occasionally hurl abuse when colleagues are out of earshot.

The photocopying ritual.

SPELL

to look ravishing on a beach holiday

Great Sun, giver of life and light,
I stand in your beams with pride.
Shine on me for this fortnight,
But let me not be fried.

Fill me with your warming shafts,
With a bikini strapped around my hips.
Endow me with such radiance,
That cellulite is eclipsed.

Great Golden Orb, Munificent Ra!
That kisses all upon the sands,
Shine on me in lands afar,
Hold me in thy glistening hands.

Rays shall glow upon my skin,
To take me beyond the pale,
And make me into a beach babe,
And not a beached whale.

SHOULD THE MAGIC FAIL:

Go snowboarding next year.

Exotic package holiday.

SPELL

to become an instant gourmet cook

Kitchen witches, come with speed!

Aid me in my hour of need.

Place the powers of your coven

Into grill and pan and oven.

Lend me all that Martha Stuart's learnt

Let my offerings be not burnt.

Make ev'ry morsel that I cook

Look as delicious as in the book.

And all that comes from within a tin

As tasty as Jamie Oliver's grin.

SHOULD THE MAGIC FAIL:

Warm the plates, call you favorite local take-out, and garnish with fresh herbs. They'll never know.

Essential utensils.

CHARM

for securing a pay rise

I maginative

N ecessary

C reative

R eliable

E nthusiastic

A mbitious

S ensational

E mployee

SPELL-CASTING TIP:

Write this charm on the back of your pay slip, wrap it around a shiny new coin and glue it to the underside of your boss's chair.

Office Polly-tricks. Best avoided.

INCANTATION

to make the bus appear

Fiddle dee dee, Fiddle dee dum,
I command the bus to come.

Fiddle dee dum, Fiddle dee dee
Appear now on the count of one, two, three!

Fiddle dee deed, Fiddle dee doad,
Vision trundle down the road!

By the aching of my feet -
Omnibus arrive, I'm feeling beat!

By the pricking of my thumbs -
A shiny bus this way comes!

SHOULD THE MAGIC FAIL:

Start walking - guaranteed to make three buses arrive at once.

Big Al drives buses.
Rides a stylish scooter on his days off.

SPELL

for rapid weight loss

Mother Earth, of bounteous flesh,
Take my girth and make it
Less. Thin my hips and
Smooth my thighs
Take me down
A dress
Size.
Nature!
Give me just
One gift - make my
Bulging buttocks lift.
Fruitful land, reclaim my
fat. Make my spare tyre go flat.

SPELL-CASTING TIP:

To be performed in the early morning light whilst offering a sacrificial chocolate biscuit to the Office Goddess.

Not recognized diet foods, but like most things (carpet included), far tastier than celery.

MANTRA

to become a word processing speed demon

Qwerty, Qwerty, Keyboard Sprite
Who latently beside me lingers,
Possess me now with all thy might;
Inhabit more than just two fingers.

Augment my quick brown fox speed
And set me free,
From lazy dog errors of typography.

Qwerty, Qwerty, Keyboard Sprite,
Indulge yourself in tapping revels.
Give my digits touch of light,
Take my output to higher levels.

From ABC to XYZ with swiftness and grace fly
To PQR and STU, but leave out RSI.

SHOULD THE MAGIC FAIL:

Casually leave brochures for voice-recognition software on the Office Manager's desk.

Tiepin. (The illustrator misinterpreted the brief.)

CHARM

for joyous living

From seed of joy so small,

Tree of happiness grow.

Bear me in your branches high,

Toward the sun of contentment.

I will on boughs of laughter dwell,

And leaves of smiles and gladness twigs

Shall nestle me in life.

SPELL-CASTING TIP:

Take a single kernel of popcorn, place in a pan with a small amount of oil. Heat with the lid on the pan, and upon hearing it pop, recite this spell.

No caption - the publisher refuses to indulge in gratuitously corny jokes.

INCANTATION

to combat washing machine demons

Spin, spin, spin-a-spun
Colors do not dare to run!

Spin, spin, spin-a-spoor
March not across the kitchen floor!

Spin, spin, spin-a-sumber
Socks, remain even in number!

Spin, spin, spin-a-spocket
Tissue, be gone from that pocket!

SHOULD THE MAGIC FAIL:

Kick the stupid machine, cry, shout, swear, scream. Then take your dirty laundry for a service wash.

Picture of the editor's underwear being dyed lilac.

CHARM

to marry the man of your dreams

The net is cast far,
The net is cast wide,
Yet this is the catch
Who will make me his bride.

Mermaids and Mermen
In this Sea of Life,
Draw the net closed
And make me his wife.

Join us in a bond
By Neptune blessed,
And let us ride forever
On love's wave crest.

SHOULD THE MAGIC FAIL:

Go for his best mate -

he's probably better looking!

Neptune: god of the sea, king of barbeques.

SPELL

to remain undetected

Secrets of nature,
Secrets of the past,
Swallow my secret,
Hold it tight and fast.

Of my deed, no bird shall sing,
None will know that it was me,
Who has done this awful thing,
I must get away scot-free.

Bury my actions deep,
Let my tracks be shameless.
Untarnished reputation keep.
I shall remain blameless.

Nonculpabilitus
Get away with it!

SHOULD THE MAGIC FAIL:

Admit full responsibility and find a good lawyer.

Illustration used earlier but just as relevant to this page and very cost-efficient.

SPELL

for harmonious bathroom relationships

Yin and Yang, Yang and Yin,
Come through the bathroom door,
Correct the imbalance there
And harmony restore.

Yin and Yang, Yang and Yin,
Toothpaste be capped and squeezed from the base,
Grimy bathtub always be rinsed,
toilet seat returned to rightful place.

Yin and Yang, Yang and Yin,
If thou wilt be my savior,
I shall never dare again
Shave my legs with his razor.

SHOULD THE MAGIC FAIL:

Put plastic wrap over the toilet seat and wait for the scream.

Many marriage therapists specialize in toothpaste related domestic conflict.

SPELL

to control unruly underwear

Briefs and thongs,

Which once were white

But grayly now are ev'ry shade of,

Amend your wrongs!

Transform aright

Into such underwear as dreams are made of.

Underwear, arise!

Underwear, arise!

Renew your ageing guise!

SHOULD THE MAGIC FAIL:

Go neo-gothic and dye all your underwear black.

Brief encounter.

CHARM

for a winning competition entry

F ly direct to the to **P**

I am a natural winne **R**

R andomly plucked from all, **I**

S end the judge a special buz **Z**

T o make his decision wis **E**

SPELL-CASTING TIP:

Write the charm in red ink underneath the postage stamp used for your entry coupon.

Unwanted prize from a prehistoric 'Spot the Pterodactyl' competition. After 65 million years of aimless wandering, he eventually found a good home with Ben Feshin, a friendly Scottish trout farmer.

INCANTATION

to afflict a love rival with a facial blemish

As I draw the magic sign

And see the face of rival mine,

The magic charm I thus opine

Will make that lightness dark.

One single zit or pustule bloom

A carbuncle of shame and gloom

The magic sign will seal this doom -

This X the spot shall mark!

SHOULD THE MAGIC FAIL:

Convince your love rival that the latest Hollywood beauty fad is a twice daily application of recycled axel grease.

Spot.

SPELL

to free your e-mail inbox from unwanted clutter

W eb around the world,
E arth lies in your broad bands.
E lectronic wizard who therein rules,
D aily, I praise your magic strands.
O blivious to this,
U ncounted people send
T waddle, nonsense, crap and junk,
J okes that never end.
U nleash me from this penury!
N et the trash and set me free!
K eep this inbox orderly.

SPELL-CASTING TIP:

Type this charm as an e-mail and send it to yourself. When it arrives, delete it straight away. DO NOT OPEN IT - the magic will be reversed and the volume of junk e-mails will triple in number.

Irritating electronic male.

SPELL

to induce laughter

Alakazam, Alakazee
Ho, ho, ho, ha ha, hee, hee

Floor to ceiling, ear to ear
Chortling, chuckling atmosphere.

Giggling grins and sparkling eyes
And great guffaws and splitting sides.

Alakazam, Alakazoom
Merry laughter fill this room!

SHOULD THE MAGIC FAIL:

Bring out your partner's childhood photo album - guaranteed to have everybody in stitches.

Einstein's undiscovered theory of no laughing matter.

INCANTATION
for perfect skin

Ye Stars that twinkle far above
Shine on my face with astral love
And let the power of thy light
Spur my crow's feet to take flight.

Cassiopeia and Sisters Seven
Bathe me in some Earthly heaven;
Lest my spots draw anguished tears,
Banish them to my teenage years.

Andromeda, I call on you
To rid my pores of grime and goo.
And Venus, bright in sky so early,
Bestow on me the cheeks of Liz Hurley.

SHOULD THE MAGIC FAIL:

Go for the paper bag option. Alternatively, lock yourself in the house and close all the curtains.

Mad Moose Miraculous Anti-Blemish Pack™: guaranteed to hide all known facial blemishes. Works in seconds.

SPELL

to read your partner's thoughts

Sing a song of sixth sense

Little pocket spy

Four and twenty hours

Inside their mind's eye

Thoughts awake and dreaming

Cannot be concealed

Fantasies, desires and needs,

All shall be revealed.

SPELL-CASTING TIP:

Croon the spell to any spider dwelling in your partner's abode. (Use with caution - it may be better not to know what your partner is thinking!)

Scientific study has proven that most people think about sex too much.

CHARM

to get the Christmas present you really, really want

Wrapping paper bright
Shrouding unknown delight
Wrap yourself round tight
The thing which I have yearned for
And will dream of tonight.

Parcels by the tree
Holding untold glee
Fill up one of thee
With the thing that I have yearned for
And dream of endlessly.

SHOULD THE MAGIC FAIL:

Make sure that you provide a comprehensive list of your preferred gifts next year to all relevant parties.

Random Christmas present of uninspiring proportions.

INCANTATION

of revenge on hairdressers

Hairdresser, it's that sad old story;
You have dethroned my crowning glory.

And as insult to this injury
I paid you to do this to me.

Nemesis! Enact my curse!
Make their hairpiece even worse.

May their highlights glow flourescent green,
And their roots for eternity be always seen.

May they live their life in hairy hell
And forever apply excess hair gel.

SHOULD THE MAGIC FAIL:

Reach for the hair clippers and go for the Sigourney Weaver in 'Alien 3' look.

Herr Gel and his amazing twitching moustache. May be booked for private parties and facial hair consultations.

SPELL

to speed up supermarket line-ups

Animal creatures of speed and swiftness
Descend upon this scene so listless.

Give the cashier the desperate need
To swipe barcodes like a cattle stampede.

Credit cards process as fast as swooping owls.
Change change hands quick as cheetah on the prowl.

Spur other shoppers to pack their wares
With the frenzied rush of mad March hares.

SHOULD THE MAGIC FAIL:

Boycott the supermarket and order all your shopping over the internet.

Matilda was a spritely 35 when she joined this supermarket line-up. The harsh reality is, that upon reaching the cashier, she will be officiously redirected to an another line-up, her basket clearly containing more than 5 items. She may never leave.

SPELL

for exam inspiration

Swot Goblin, who spake in Einstein's ear,

Speak in my ear now.

Swot Goblin, who in Da Vinci's mind dwelt

Come dwell upon my brow.

Swot Goblin, lay your knowledge down

In my brain so hot and flurried

And give me all the facts I need

E'en though my cramming was hurried.

My pen be filled with wisdom's ink,

Swot Goblin, make me think, think, think!

SPELL-CASTING TIP:

To be mouthed silently in your moment of greatest need with hands placed over your face whilst rocking slowly backwards and forwards in your chair.

Beware: rocking in your chair may attract unwanted attention.

MANTRA

to pick lucky lottery numbers

Number of glory,

Number of joy,

Number of liberty,

Number of hope,

Number of freedom,

Number of dreams.

Numbers I mark,

Numbers I call,

Numbers appear

On each lucky ball!

SPELL-CASTING TIP:

Recite this charm quickly, waving a pen anticlockwise, and randomly mark a number on your lottery slip after each wave of the pen.

Life: a lottery.

INCANTATION

to win an argument

No disputation

No complication

No elaboration

No reparation

No prolongation

No arbitration

No more heated conversation

Know the truth of the situation

I am right!

SHOULD THE MAGIC FAIL:

Admit defeat, be sweetness and light, then accidentally pour cold gravy into the boots of the argumentative person in question.

Expensive camera filled with raspberry jam.

CHARM

to deter the onset of baldness

(You may choose to show this to your partner.)

Oh Great Full Moon so round and gleaming
Stop my hairline from receeding.

Ye who bids seas ebb and flow,
Turn the tide, make my hair grow.

Ye who puts werewolves in pursuit,
Make me just a little more hirsute.

Ye who monthly wane and wax,
Adorn my pate with what it lacks.

From retirement, please do save my comb.
Make my head less like the Millennium Dome.

SHOULD THE MAGIC FAIL:

Give in gracefully and invest in a baseball cap.

Many bald men buy fast cars with money saved on haircuts.

SPELL

to prevent a run in your tights

Hocus Pocus, leg appeal,
Imbue my tights with strength of steel.

Mumbo, Jumbo, pins so stunning,
Let my limbs do all the running.

Kazam, Kazoo, shield me from my dread,
Ladder, stay in backyard shed.

Hocus, Pocus, one wish solely,
Keep my hosiery unholy.

SHOULD THE MAGIC FAIL:

Forget the tights and show a bit of leg.

A recent survey revealed that no less than 82.6% of motor mechanics regularly wear tights beneath their overalls.

SPELL

for finding evasive possessions

Turnabout, roundabout
Show me the whereabouts
Of the item gone astray
Relocate and unmislay.

Turnabout, roundabout
Stop me tearing my hair out,
Hunting Spirits be my guides
Disclose, reveal where it hides.

Find, and lift me from dejection,
Point me in the right direction!

SPELL-CASTING TIP:

This spell should be chanted whilst spinning around on the spot with your eyes closed. The direction you face when the spell is complete is the direction in which you should begin your search.

Metal detectors: generally not very useful when looking for your car in a busy parking lot.

CHARM

to stop your partner snoring

Breathe long, breathe deep,
Breathe soft in sleep.

Breathe calm, breathe cute,
No pig, you brute.

Breathe long, breathe wide,
Lie on your side.

Breathe soft, breathe low;
I need sleep too, you know.

SPELL-CASTING TIP:

To be recited whilst waving freshly crushed garlic over your sleeping partner's face.

The Mad Moose No-more-snore Kit™
(Available at all good anti-snore stores.)

SPELL
to keep houseplants alive

Nymphs of Spring, cross my threshold,
Come from dale and hill.
Frolic in my domicile
With Alan Titchmarsh skill.
Bring leafy life to my domain,
The withered stems that are my shame,
Wilt no more, but thrive!

Nymphs of Spring, come with thumbs green,
Answer this fertile calling,
Save the stalks and leaves and buds
From a fate appalling.
Tend them as a growing daughter
Though I may forget to water
Let them all survive!

SHOULD THE MAGIC FAIL:

Buy low maintenance greenery: a cactus or a bunch of plastic roses.

For those of you who are unaware, Alan Titchmarsh is the UK's No.1 horticultural genius and vegetation guru. He has written many books on gardening, none of which we have published and are therefore not obliged to promote in any way whatsoever.

CHARM

to squeeze into a busy parking lot

Abracardabra
I have sought far and near;
Of a gap there is no trace.

Abracardabra
The enchanted way is clear;
For everything there is a place.

Abracardabra
Cross the final frontier;
Find this car a space!

SPELL-CASTING TIP:

Perform whilst driving around in circles in your chosen parking lot. At least six circuits should be completed before the magic will begin to take effect.

Selection of global animal-aware roadsigns unlikely to be encountered in your local supermarket parking lot.

SPELL

to get rid of a cold

Winds of corners four,
I call on you to blow
Down this nose, red raw,
To rid me of this woe.

North wind, South wind, East and West,
Billow cold and billow hot,
Gust with warmth of thermal vest,
Out, out damned snot.

Hurricane and cyclone whirl
In caressing tender breeze,
In that endless dancing twirl
I place this draughty sneeze!

SPELL-CASTING TIP:

A genuine sneeze should be emitted when reciting the final line of this spell. Repeat the final line continuously until the sneeze is forthcoming.

Random 'gorilla tactics' illustration.

INCANTATION

to ensure your punctual arrival

Clock, tock, tickety-tick
Hear this, quickety-quick
Now stop, lickety-split
Hold your hands apace.

Time, mine, tackety-tack
Which I lackety-lack
Speed my trackety-track
Onward in this race.

My head's, tockety-tock
On the blockety-block
Give the boss a shockety-shock
Early in work place!

SHOULD THE MAGIC FAIL:

Be sure to leave a jacket on the back of your chair every night so it appears as if you are in early for a meeting, even if you're still in bed.

Spot. Possesses the rare ability to bark the time using the 24-hour clock. Squeals indicate that it's half past the hour or that somebody has trodden on his tail.

CHARM

to increase willpower

(Particularly useful when trying to break a habit, e.g. smoking, nail-biting or eating pickles.)

Metals of the Earth
Nuggets, veins and ores,
Lend me all your strength,
Alloy me to my cause.
Lead and bronze and tin
Lying far below,
Lend me all your strength
I must not bend or bow.
Will of Iron! Will of Steel!
Stand me firm through this ordeal!

SHOULD THE MAGIC FAIL:

Clean the house to take your mind off your obsession! If you've been trying to give up cleaning, then all is lost.

Do not trust this man - he lies compulsively.

INCANTATION

to rid running shoes of noxious odors

South Wind, blow fresh and blow sweet,
Blow toxic fumes away from my feet.

Let perfume arise from whence it stank
In the dark depths of these sneakers dank.

Of noxious gases remove all traces
So in public I may untie my laces.

Billow me along on scented cloud,
Of trendy footwear make me rightly proud.

Though sweat and time must take their toll,
Lift this dreaded curse, and cleanse my sole.

SHOULD THE MAGIC FAIL:

Put your running shoes outside the front door where they can double as an effective burglar deterrent.

Offensive biological material - disturbingly outside the remit of the Geneva Convention.

SPELL

of silence

(Useful for noisy children or drunken husbands.)

With a peck of hush and a pinch of calm
You will fall under my charm.

When I touch you with my magic finger
No more shall this hubbub linger.

Dissonance and cacophony cease!
Keep Mum happily in peace!

Midas Power, be born anew!
Silence is golden - and so are you!

SHOULD THE MAGIC FAIL:

Buy a drum kit and drown them all out.

Va Moose. Reputed to have broken the sound barrier at least once.

SPELL

to keep your head when all about are losing theirs

Crisis, Disaster, Catastrophe,
Everything has hit the fan.

Fiasco, Breakdown, Emergency,
The Boss has turned the color of spam.

Yet red-faced screams do not solutions make
And this turmoil and panic is more than I can take,

Hence, now from me, with the wisdom that I know,
Let soothing, calming oil on these troubled waters flow.

SPELL-CASTING TIP:

An olive should be chewed while performing this spell. It is therefore advisable to always have a small jar of this magic fruit about your person.

This man once lost his head. Fortunately he discovered the "Spell for finding evasive possessions" on page 74.

INCANTATION

to rekindle an old flame

Will o' the Wisp, glide in from the fen,

Flicker in his breast again,

Weave and dart and tease his soul

Fol-di-ree, Fol-di-rol

Will o' the Wisp, lure him on,

Spark up where you once had gone

Fol-di-rol, Fol-di-ree

Guide his love-thoughts back to me.

SPELL-CASTING TIP:

Chant at the witching hour whilst holding a candle by an open window. Note: bright orange socks must be worn.

Three solvent singles.
All have own hare and car.

Other titles in this range include:

A SURPRISINGLY SOOTHING BOOK OF HARMONY FOR THOSE TEETERING ON THE BRINK OF TOTAL NEUROTIC MELTDOWN

AN INCREDIBLY ILLUMINATING BOOK OF DREAMS FOR THOSE WHO BELIEVE THAT ALL SUBCONSCIOUS THOUGHTS ARE REALLY ABOUT SEX